ZUGZWANG: A POETRY COLLECTION

By: Denice Lovett

Zugzwang

/ˈzəɡˌzwaNG, ˈtso͞oɡˌtsvaNG/
noun: zugzwang

1. A situation in chess in which a player is forced to move a piece into a bad position, especially one from which the piece will be lost.[1]

2. Here in these pages, it shall be drawn upon as the Intersectional scope used to both view and solve contemporary American social and political issues as a Black woman. Ex: "If a move is made as a Black woman for equality, the potential for a disadvantage or loss of voice may seem more likely than not."

---

[1] n/a. (2022). *Zugzwang*. zugzwang noun - Definition, pictures, pronunciation and usage notes | Oxford Advanced Learner's Dictionary at OxfordLearnersDictionaries.com. Retrieved September 12, 2022, https://www.oxfordlearnersdictionaries.com/us/definition/english/zugzwang?q=zugzwang.

Double Consciousness

1. Double-consciousness is a concept in social philosophy referring, originally, to a source of inward "twoness" putatively experienced by African Americans because of their racialized oppression and devaluation in a white-dominated society. The concept is often associated with William Edward Burghardt Du Bois, who introduced the term into social and political thought, famously, in his groundbreaking political insight of The Souls of Black Folk (1903).[2]

---

[2] J. P., Pittman (2016, March 21). *Double consciousness*. Stanford Encyclopedia of Philosophy. Retrieved September 12, 2022, https://plato.stanford.edu/entries/double-consciousness/

PART ONE

"Warning, in music-words devout and large, we are each other's harvest: we are each other's business: we are each other's magnitude and bond."

—Gwendolyn Brooks, *Paul Robeson*

Shall I Name the Earth?

They call the hillsides mama because
Her soft curves and sweet caress
hug the wide-open fields of weeds and burnt grass.
She is what revitalizes life and death—
Her bosom as brown as the ones
before her, her core filled with
black jagged slate,
long-ago felt feelings of racism
before she placed her hand
upon the freedom gates.
Her grass was long and waved in the wind
but at her roots crabgrass began
to peak out at the sky as
a touch of Her curl reminds me of
Her ride, Her journey, walked with a certain
pride and stride that mirrors the lively
stream passing through and beside
the rounded edges of Her hillsides,
the mind that saw too much for Her to
tell me why she won't talk about the
erosion of Her body due to mudslides
waterboarding Her thoughts and deceiving Her eyes.

They call the hillsides mama, because
She brought forth a new way of life.

Music.

The music of the universe is everywhere.
It's beautiful in its mundane quality.
In fact, do some of us search our whole lives for it,
only to speak over such plain beauties,
that when an artist, musician or poet presents us with sheet
music,
do we become shocked?

If we instead just tilted our heads to the left a bit,
we could hear the audible lessons that were otherwise
diminished.
Therefore, we ourselves would be in the position
of the artist, poet, or musician.
Sure, some would yell at us to get our heads out of the clouds,
but it'll be too hard to face reality without the music.

Landmark case of Love v. Fear

What has more power—
Love or Fear?

Love conquers all
but fear can
stagnate in the hearts of all.

Maybe love drives fear
for if not fear
there'd be none to hold closer—
or—fear drives love
to be determined a hellish
and a joyous rollercoaster.

Fear and love, love and fear.
One should not have power over
the other one here.
For Ying doesn't Yang without
Yang to caress Ying.
Love is quite fearing
and to fear for others
is to be loving.

Conversation in the Park

Approaching me with two crème sodas, they subtly cussed—

"It's too peaceful of a day."
"…Meaning?"

"The world is up to something. Maybe we'll find out how devious tomorrow."

Night In The Mine

The steady thrumming of Cassia's heart
served as the bass for
the canary's song,
causing a queer harmony to arise.

The canary's song weakened
In smoke-soaked darkness,
sharp wings beating out of time
fast 'round the room of shame,
knocking into Cassia's consciousness
and hovering to hide the stains
of anxiety beneath flitted shadows.

Cassia lie trapped neath the linen cover,
flushed tight between her legs
clawing up her back
and grasping at her neck ,
bounding her body to earth
rather than to soul.

Her soul was never meant to go that easy,
though became a quirky
bearer of witness—
thrust bolt upright
into the blue-black sky—
seeing fist reach toward
the now split spectator
amongst realms beginning to collapse
in tandem to final tug North,
all seeking first prize.
Fright and fury came fast to her soul
for it was to beat
it's ultimate captor,

bypassing fingertips and
screeching downward in the final throe—
drawing closer to Cassia's mouth
blowing flames upward,
lit by inner hellfire in death's face.
Mind chirping in harmony with the bird,
bloodshot eyes forced to open
like hands upon Gabriel's Gate,
Cassia freed herself from deaths
rough thread bare grip.
The eve never waned as did not
the glimpses of the wings on the canary.

You Hear Me Calling?

Curious Herald is history.

Here I am,

fate dared woman

telling in being

scarce in a man's world

while trumpets blare

falsely at my black hands.

How delusional humanity must be.

Pater

What punishments of God are not Gifts?[3]
I sit in the place of heretic,
bound by pride's fleeting thoughts.
They whisper healing to my heartbreak
caused by God, for He bent me backward
to the breaking point—
long weary of hot times arising anew
like Mountain Laurel once burned in bellum.

I am made in His image a harsh veneration.
The humanity in The Knowing—
of trapped disadvantage
yet the mere hope for
collective advancement—
is now the punishment I possess,
placed within me by God in hellish secret.

It is a telling illusion of choice and freedom
that I am nothing special amongst righteous mortals.
I am simply the means to the end of their self-suffering.

---

[3] Mostly Water. (2019, August 17). *Stephen Colbert and Anderson Cooper's beautiful conversation about grief*. The Stephen Colbert Interview. Retrieved September 13, 2022, https://www.youtube.com/watch?v=YB46h1koicQ.

What We Lost

Can we reach the end—
the far-away light around the bend?

Will the fear strike us so
that we'll freeze in space with nowhere to go?

Each of our lips stuck together, unable to yell
to scream out a warning, an alarm, an admittance bell.

Our arms outstretched to grab at the darkness
scratching and climbing to reach freedom's assist.

May they move swift enough to unlock my lips,
slowly pull up my body and guide along my hips.

Feet now unstuck but still heavily weighted,
may the light our fingers tickle leave us placated.

Our spirits shall move forward our bodies
for the end result shall be too shocking.

For the light we seek was never lost,
it was to be snatched from within us.

Where to Go

Change is the only

constant progress, never far from

disappointment.

PART TWO

"I have come to believe, over and over again, that what is most important to me must be spoken, made verbal and shared, even at the risk of having it bruised or misunderstood."

—Audre Lorde, *Sister Outsider*

"For the master's tools will never dismantle the master's house. They may allow us temporarily to beat him at his own game, but they will never enable us to bring about genuine change."

—Audre Lorde, *The Master's Tools Will Never Dismantle The Master's House*

Not All About Me

My faith is not exact to yours, you see,
but I've wanted to understand both
yours and mine in my mind's eye before
pursed lips breath critique—
speaking before thinking—
about how far we've come yet
there's still a lot left to beat.

My words are not your words you see,
there's a difference in my tongue's
slip of cheek—
sweet yet bitter, kind and sharp—
I walk a fine line between
what you assume I'll say
and what I actually speak
because fear of others does not make lasting peace.

Still my oppression exists you see,
I wear it clenched around my mind
begging others to set me free—
from being born into this depth of difference
created to separate you from me—

My searching feet have walked the same miles as you
you see, but I find that the quality
of my souls have waned and taught me
how to stand,

how to be.

Central Valley (Part I)

I let my ego flit in quandary
over my hometown—she's atypical of my people,
though she's aware of me
as she lays dormant, not in haste,
to cause fraudulent accusations.
She instead strikes slyly at her own convenience,
only wanting to balance out
the status quo when necessary—
an eye for an eye if you will.

Nuzzled shadow laden neath Blue Ridge,
her head in hands rest in
blood-soaked farmland woolen men of
civil blockades and fixed bayonets
bestowed upon her.
She gazed briefly upon the siege,
only shutting them to sleep when abettors
of divided Manifest Destiny lay claim upon her.

But alas, once she awoke to present day,
bearing witness to new duellum bellum house fire
she chose to stay stuck in her righteous place,
far from Brotherly Love,
taking cover under Tuscarora.

She's been self-inquisitive yet outwardly silent since—
reminding herself to stay grounded in
her Quaker ideals of Trusting in Equality of all men—
for there is a fresh bounty to be reaped by all friends.
Still intrusive thought interrupts
as memories of centuries past
flood forth to her attention,
as she seems finally aware

that she has only allowed communion
with one type of people outside of her heritage…

Small Town

I live in a place where church steeples and old silos stand as
high as skyscrapers.
Where the bright neon lights are outshone by the orange
sunset
to the billboards of the Appalachia towering over above us,
is where our eyes wonder to take in their headlines.
A hawk's apartment rests in the penthouse of a maple tree
and the tenants below him use browned corn stocks to secure
their balconies.
Taxi's down below are green and big-wheeled,
splattered with manure instead of a Broadway production.

I live in a place where grass is sometimes used
as a crosswalk to get from point A to B.
Where cows outcompete lengthy car alarms
and their exhaust stays in the walls of households only a few
blocks away.
Where brooks, rivers, and streams are just as active as traffic
during mid-day.
Where mom and pop store's chalkboard advertisements
run together in heaps like garbage on the sidewalk,
beckoning some to come and shop
yet subtly refusing service to others
by following them—brown folk 'round the store.
eyes rest on the newcomer not knowing she's a townie,
cut sideways to catch her stealing, even though
she's gonna pay full price and be "thankful" for her experience
smiling wide to dissipate mistrust and holding her receipt in her
hand as she leaves, just in case security wants to double
check.
Her affected, "Thank you, goodbye!"
is matched with a smug "Bye.".

I live in a place where a rural town bustling like a city,
a place I called home,
a place that I'm forever tied to.
But I am forever aware of the undertones of my reality,
It's made this way purposefully up here.
In the South they'll just kill you.
But in the North, they'll get you to kill yourself.[4]

---

[4] Imani Barbarin or @crutches_and_spice on TikTok. The video I referenced has since been taken down by the app, but her articles can be found at https://www.patreon.com/ImaniBarbarin/posts

Broke Down Sonnet

Shall I whisper truths to thine soul?
For you being a man made of kkkloth
in disguise and independent control—
you might not know thoughts of dark swath.

As a rising tide of spited youth,
gain populace in rights unpaid
thy come unearthed to system tableau—
an erasure of slave homes racists made.

Given selves empty life and liberty,
Sold land and made money—killed.
Yet weary of swords shadow from head to feet.
Entitled to spoils for crowning good heals.

Though thoughts of uprising stay close mind,
For White maleness ruling is out of time.

Begotten

I am a legacy
I come from the seventy[5]
I'm built with the remedy—
mDNA you can't see.
Build up walls, make profits offa me.
Make sense, set sail,
beat, kill,
rape, jail, seek prophets outta me.

Sexualize, objectify, distort, distrust.
A female black body, a black soul, a black voice,
a deep rich nation washed in misogyny.
I reteach, remake, I retake,
retell in detail my bloodline,
Non-homogenized
the truth is that the
truth needs to not die.

Feed my mind so I can lead
or strive to try.
So, I can't leave this Earth the same,
reminded to be the peace everlasting
arise anew Regina project,
new legacy, 'cause that broke male shit
almost fucked up the whole scheme.

---

[5] Musixmatch . (2021, August 24). *Family Ties by Baby Keem featuring Kendrick Lamar*. AZLyrics.com. Retrieved September 23, 2022, from
https://www.azlyrics.com/lyrics/babykeem/familyties.html.

Zugzwang

Yesterday was heavy
So, I let it fall to the floor.
Roe v. Wade has gone away
and with it a new feminist rage
has caught fire.
Bodily autonomy is where
Red hot heads have hit the ceiling.

We warned you.
We knew it was coming for us—
not you White men,
for you're the Devil I know.
I mean you White women,
new moderate centers of the show.

You're awfully late.

Central Valley (Part II)

…for her mind is fueled by coal fodder forged,
stopping only to notice a shift in her winds,
in the people that inhabit around her.
While she peers between bated breath watching me
from high above, she questions my ancestry.
My audacity to step free feet beneath her
without fear of being flogged—

(though she will find another way,
perhaps through mind games and trickery.)

She must think "How dare I let my sight be clouded
by my dark history, brought forth by familiar dark people."

Yes—how did I—a Blue, Black, Catholic,
filter into her view?
Her majestic manifestation quilt of Red, Whites, and lush
green?
How dare I stand atop her—
sweet darling Kittatinny,
and speak of her loathsome qualities
spawned in her youth?
How dare I call her home yet
never run from her wickedness?

She only asked of the dark history to deter—
I will it of her in order to forgive.
To remember the pain she has caused,
To grieve it and let it go.
To find peace and light in all of her people,

For they move forever around and beneath
And she is stuck with both their
consequences and their rewards.
She needs them all to stay stable
to remain alive as an earthly wonder.

Reciprocal Zugzwang

Women of color and disabled women
have been organizing for over two hundred years.
Been tested by, tested on,
killed by dr. j. marion sims,
pregnant and held between countries
with little to no care—
neglected by our government
because we can tolerate more pain,
because being born here sometimes
feels like a self-inflicted sin.

We're forced into sub-standard livings
because we're not "normal" and
that's what is deserved—
to be infantilized, patronized, invisible and unheard.
We go missing on res land,
beaten to death and then forgotten.
We're mowed down by gunman at
an Atlanta spa just because being Asian
to him was to be sexually tempting.
To be trans, queer or non-binary
to those who choose to murder
because they're confused about themselves
and take it out violently on our loved ones.

Yes, yesterday was heavy.
The tipping point for you.
Meanwhile, all of this was happening in
our shared community.
Happening to BIPOC and LGBTQIA women and non-binaries
who begged, hell—*pleaded* to their deaths for help.

For your help.
Now we must all hold space in the center for White women.
And you know we have to, that we must,
And you'll wonder why we're not grateful for your presence.

This is hard work, not a fleeting resonance.
It's heavy lifting for a lifetime, minimum.

So, I hope you caught yesterday when I dropped it,
and I hope you don't make up for lost time slowly.

In the meantime, please ask yourselves this question,
just to see if you're ready:

As a White Woman, am I oppressed enough to not know my
privilege,
or am I privileged enough to weaponize it?

Memo

"Why did you write that?"
"You're only hurting yourself."
"You seem angry."
"You seem bitter."
"You're not passionate about feminism."
"You always talk about race,
like I like your work but,
you could talk about anything else."
"You don't know what you're talking about."
"Why is this about me?"
"You're setting back the movement
by being accusatory."
"You're a mean, bitter, Black bitch."

These are comments told to me
as a Black female poet,
by White folks via projection.
Or should I say stubbornness.
Stubbornness which often times
is deafening to truths you need to hear.

If White people cannot handle
the truth that I write,
if they continue to project these
words of guilt and anger
onto me and onto my work,
if I let it be so,
they'll achieve their goal of
never doing the necessary emotional,
mental and physical race work—
they'll continue to outsource it to me
in order to live blissfully in their comfort zone
of White Supremacy.

Go figure.

I'm not doing the work for you—rather,
I'm not doing the heavy lifting anymore.
I'm not moved by your comments,
not shocked by the subtle racism and misogyny,
quite frankly, it's become disappointing.
It's no longer about me and my work,
It's about you finally sitting with your feelings.

It's about time you deal with your
creation and contempt of race.

Defeat

Why do I always shudder at the word "defeat"?
I guess, to me, it doesn't really register as just a word.
It registers as an emotion,
A psychological route towards believing
that you just aren't good enough.

But why must defeat cripple me?
why should it chew me up inside
and spit out half-assed justifications
that mask behavior everyone else thinks,
"wasn't your best."
"You'll never be first, even if you work hard."

I thought I worked hard.
I thought I out worked everyone.
I thought I did my best.
I thought I did my greatest.
I thought I earned a win.

How do I accept defeat
while handling all other criticisms
that are continuously yelled in my ear and thrive?
how shall I keep progressing in the face of all this?

Answer: Answers may vary.

Answer: Because I choose me anyway.
I choose my best self over outer validation and critique
anyway.
I choose to radically be right and wrong without fault-finding
Before others do so or reassure me that it isn't so.
What I will not do is bow to narcissism,
for that is projection to others tenfold

not safety for me in mind nor morals.

I am self-aware, gracious and self-kind,
I am a rising victor over self-defeat.

PART THREE

"To truly love, we must learn to mix various ingredients—care, affection, recognition, respect, commitment, and trust, as well as honest and open communication."

—bell hooks, *All About Love: New Visions*

Watchful Creed

I am not just "America" objectified.
I am his forethought,
the bearer of his past,
the brunt of his present.
I am the summation 246—
nay 403 years of disgust,
of irritation at himself.
At his insecurity of personal integrity
and it's ties to his whiteness.
Over time I've become both his morality
gauge and witness,
victim and scapegoat.

All because I write the truth
he most definitely doesn't wish to see—
it's another reminder of his existence being futile
the razor with which hangs above him dipping slowly
downward—
inflaming his fixation on secrets that made him King,
and projecting them outward onto me.
Yet, despite the brushes against
all truths seen and heard,
at every turn he denies
himself a path to enlightenment.

That frustration he has becomes my problem.
Yet he is all knowing,
light from light
dark from dark
begotten and made lawfully
consubstantial with only his freedom
all of "America" was made.

New Negro Attitude

Oh, the Joy! Oh, the crime!
Oh, what a time to be alive!

Each day we face the rising sun,
of our new day begun wondering
what will happen when
the UV Rays hit our faces—
a perfect mixture of glinting gold, rich chocolate, and history—
surely jealousy may arise along
with hate and fear in some eyes.

Oh, the joy! Oh, the crime!

To be black in America is to cause tension to arise—
we must maintain our individuality in a unique civilization—
to be aligned with their God and their nation,
to be invisible yet visible in closed-door conversations.
How predictable. How boring.

Oh, what a time to be alive!

A votive to black struggle, black power,
black pride in the skin we wear, the curl of our hair,
the sway of our walks,
the hindrance of our talk—
Oh, what a joy! Oh, what a crime!
Oh, what a time to be alive!

Self

What about me?
My Blackness?
My gender?
My oppression?
The answer lies within the questions;
I am me—
a Black woman
I am a person double oppressed.
But I am not palatable
to my oppressor.
My weaknesses prescribed to my identity
by white people are simply
freeing to my soul.
I am foreign to them yet am American made.
They brought me here to rock
their world and make their planet twirl[6]—
I am the future.
I rest in innovation and unlearned knowledge
given by the oppressor.
I am the shit.
I'mma keep doing me.

So, what about me?

---

[6] Blavity TV. (2020, March 20). *How to Scale Access & Outcomes in Media: Erica Alexander & Tracy Oliver | AT Main Stage Talks*. YouTube. Retrieved September 25, 2022. https://www.youtube.com/watch?v=dwYdpeMdHac

Haiku for 2023

It's really simple.

Black women are humans.

That's it. That's the poem.

Vacation

If I could wake up anywhere,
It would be on a white sand beach,
in a church white wooden house,
amongst milky colored walls,
with billowy virgin white lace
curtains blowing against the European white
bed frame, and French flat white
bedspread as

a   Black   mass
of
power,
pride,
sense and sensibility
in myself and my clear

contrast against the world around me—
a place which has a bit more peace in my imagination

than
in my
reality

In Summation

The sum of my humanity
Isn't just love, fear, rage, repeat.
My humanity consists of love,
Humor, sadness, mistakes, anger,
Knowledge, loyalty, respect, kindness,
Creativity, compassion and gratitude.
How perplexing yet brilliant is being.

A Guide to Prepare the Mind for Moonlight

Step 1: Go outside into the darkness
rest your body amongst the pine trees—
let the warm summer breeze carry the scent down
to your nose and into your lungs,
the sap sticking to the sides of your skull
to numb unrelenting thoughts of yesterday, today and
tomorrow.

Step 2: Face the moon to bathe as much as possible
in the light that shall baptize your dreams—
your uncontrollable ocean of repetitious mindlessness
progresses.

Step 3: Close your eyes and feel the light on your lids
the finger-touch from the mother moon above,
singing to you gently an abundant hymn,
"Go forth my child and live life on a whim—"

Step 4: "—For life is too short to stand here
and bask in my far-reaching song…"
You open your eyes, now recharged
and motivated as

Step 5: to travel into the new darkness
of your bedroom and escape to a dreamy wanderlust.

Quietness

In the sunshine-golden haze of late August,
Quietness has come out to play—
though the sweet Peonies
and Weeping Willow tassels sway
rustling along with the incessant Robin bouncing
and crisply chirping between them.
The wind acts swiftly then them all—
blowing with slightly more force,
that it eventually wraps around my head
like a scarf round my ears,
stifling the flora and fauna
from coming all quickly my way,
bringing me silence, pure bliss,
in ever slipping quiet.

Trash "Men"

I wonder about the collectors
of my now tossed memories,
hopes, dreams, and emotions.

The human beings
who sifted through texts such as
Beloved,
Slouching Towards Bethlehem,
The Bible—
and my 3rd grade diary
where I felt the need to use as many curse words as
there were vowels present.

They're trying to find something meaningful
enough to satisfy their appetites,
for their own left them starved
to find something new and fruitful.
I appreciate the notion that
they'd find some treasure in my thrown away thoughts.

I hope that the men, women, and non-binary
pick all of them up,
stuff them inside the pockets of their minds
and leave them there to rest—
to become the place where my life is kept,
for I have few other places to fully exist.

FIN

Acknowledgements

I would like to extend my deepest thanks to all those who have accompanied me on this poetic journey. The creation of this book has been an arduous and soul-stirring undertaking, and I could not have done it without the unyielding support, guidance, and inspiration of those around me.

Foremost among these cherished individuals are my family, whose unwavering love of debate on everything from current geopolitical critical issues to pop culture helped fine tune my voice. This along with the life-long encouragement to further educate myself in and out of school have sustained me through the trials and tribulations of life. Their presence in my life has been a constant guidepost and source of love.

Equally instrumental have been my friends, whose sage advice, empathetic listening, and unwavering support have lifted me up when I needed it most, and whose unwavering faith in my artistic vision has been a beacon of hope and inspiration.

The guidance and mentorship of my fellow writers, teachers/professors and creative allies have also been critical to my growth as a poet. Their boundless wisdom, honesty, artistic vision, and unshakeable belief in the power of words have emboldened me to take risks, explore new horizons, and push the boundaries of my craft.

Finally, I wish to express my heartfelt gratitude to my readers, whose unwavering support and engagement have been a constant source of inspiration and motivation. Your passion for the written word has given me the courage to continue embarking on this poetic journey, and for this, I am eternally grateful.

Bibliography

Barbarin, Imani or @crutches_and_spice on TikTok. The video
I referenced has since
been taken down by the app, but her articles can be
found at
https://www.patreon.com/ImaniBarbarin/posts

Blavity TV. (2020, March 20). How to Scale Access &
Outcomes in Media: Erica
Alexander & Tracy Oliver: AT Main Stage Talks.
YouTube. Retrieved September 25,
2022. https://www.youtube.com/watch?v=dwYdpeMdH
ac

Mostly Water. (2019, August 17). Stephen Colbert and
Anderson Cooper's beautiful
conversation about grief. The Stephen Colbert
Interview. Retrieved September 13, 2022,
https://www.youtube.com/watch?v=YB46h1koicQ

Musixmatch . (2021, August 24). Family Ties by Baby Keem
featuring Kendrick Lamar.
AZLyrics.com. Retrieved September 23, 2022, from
https://www.azlyrics.com/lyrics/babykeem/familyties.ht
ml.

n/a. (2022). Zugzwang. zugzwang noun - Definition, pictures,
pronunciation and usage
notes, Oxford Advanced Learner's Dictionary at
OxfordLearnersDictionaries.com. Retrieved
September 12, 2022,
https://www.oxfordlearnersdictionaries.com/us/definitio
n/english/zugzwang?q=zugzwang

Pittman, J. P. (2016, March 21). Double consciousness. Stanford Encyclopedia

Philosophy. Retrieved September 12, 2022, https://plato.stanford.edu/entries/double-consciousness/

CPSIA information can be obtained
at www.ICGtesting.com
Printed in the USA
LVHW052122140723
752119LV00013B/992